After The Beginning
The Play

by
Sue L. Adkins

Sue L. Adkins

Illustrations by Ann-Michelle Courtney Ross Molinar
Cover Colorizations by Paula Rusk

ISBN 0-9672605-7-4
Copyright 1999 Cheudi Publishing
International Copyright Secure. All rights reserved including performing rights. WARNING! This play is protected by Copyright law. Anyone who reproduces copyright matter is subject to substantial penalties and assessments for each infringement.

Printed in the U.S.A.
10 9 8 7 6 5 4 3 2 1

ROYALITY NOTE

Possession of this book (e-book or hard copy) without written authorization first having been obtained from the publisher, confers no right or license, to professionals or amateurs, to produce the play, publicly or in private, for gain or charity. However, productions of this play are encouraged, and those who wish to present it may secure the necessary permission from Cheudi Publishing, Plano, Texas 75094, USA.

Professional producers are requested to apply to Cheudi Publishing for Royalty quotation.

This play may be presented by amateurs, upon payment to Cheudi Publishing of a royalty (to be determined) for each performance, one week before the date the play is to be given. The play is fully protected by copyright, and anyone presenting the play without the consent of Cheudi Publishing, will be liable to penalties provided by the copyright law.

Each time the play is produced, the name of the author must be carried in all publicity, advertising, fliers, and programmes.

After The Beginning The Play

Table of Contents

ACT I

SCENE I

SCENE II

SCENE III

SCENE IV

SCENE V

PRODUCTION INFORMATION

Sue L. Adkins

Note From The Author

No one knows what went on in the Garden after Eden after Adam and Eve were sent away forever. What happened to the animals? Who took care of them? It must have been a scary time. This is the first of a series of stories about the three animal friends. In this story three friends decide to go to a far off, forbidden place. There they meet a scary monster. Two manage to escape and one is captured. Village friends must go to the rescue. We learn that we should not accept everything we see; and we must not listen to those who try to get us to do wrong. When we do it can lead to big trouble. We have to stay strong and do what is right.

This play tells us that it is good to obey and tell the truth. We must pray, and be ready to forgive. Examples are told in story and songs. We pray these lessons will become part of the lives of all who read, perform, see, and hear this work. We hope it makes you think and influences you and others in a positive way.

Sue L. Adkins

ACT I

SCENE I

(*VILLAGERS ENTER, WAVE, GREET; WORK; PRUNE; WATER PLANTS*)

CROWD: "HELLO! GOOD MORNING! WHAT A BEAUTIFUL DAY!"

LION: "YES! WONDERFUL!"

MRS. ELEPHANT: "AND THE BEST TIME OF THE MORNING!"

SONG: IN OUR GARDEN

(SOME *VILLAGERS EXIT, OTHERS STAY, MIME TALK, SWEEP, WATER PLANTS. O.D. ENTERS, X TO TREE, PICKS FRUIT, VILLAGERS XDR AND BECOME THE CHORUS. MOTHER ENTERS, STOPS O. D. FROM EATING FRUIT*)

MOTHER: "O.D! STOP!"

O.D: "W-WHAT?"

MOTHER: "REMEMBER WHAT *HE* TOLD THE HUMANS?"

O. D. POSSUM: "W-WHO?" *(LOOKS AROUND)*

MOTHER: "YOU KNOW!"

O. D. POSSUM: "UH-H," *(THINKS, SHURGS)*

MOTHER: "HE TOLD THEM NOT TO EAT THE FRUIT FROM THIS TREE!" *(PAUSE)* "DO YOU KNOW WHAT THEY DID!"

O. D. *(SHURGS)* "THEY ATE IT?"

MOTHER: "YES! SHE ATE," *(O. D'S PUZZLED)*

O. D. "OH-H." *(SHRUGS)*

(VILLAGERS ENTER)

MOTHER: "HE ATE THE FRUIT AND, OH-H…!" *(SHAKES HER HEAD)*

O.D: "WHAT HAPPENED?"

MOTHER: *(SAD)* "GOD PUT THEM OUT OF THE GARDEN."

O. D. "OH-H."

MOTHER SINGS:
DON'T EAT THE FRUIT

MOTHER: "AND DO YOU SEE ANY HUMANS HERE?"

O. D: "NO."

MOTHER: "WE MUST DO WHAT GOD SAYS. FRUIT FROM THE TREE IN

THE MIDDLE IS FORBIDDEN!"

(O. D *NODS, PUTS FRUIT DOWN, SITS, LISTENS AS MOTHER AND CHORUS SING)*

SONG: OBEY THE LORD

MOTHER: "I HAVE TO GO HELP

YOUR FATHER GATHER FOOD.
PLAY WITH YOUR FRIENDS UNTIL I
GET BACK."

O. D. "YES MA'AM."

MOTHER: "OH, AND DON'T GO TO
THE EASTSIDE!" *(CALLS)* "PHILLIP!
VIOLET!"

O. D: "THE EASTSIDE?"

MOTHER: *(NODS)* "NEVER GO THERE!
(CALLS) "PHILLIP! VIOLET!"

PHILLIP & VIOLET: "YES MA'AM?"
(PHILLIP AND VIOLET ENTER)

MOTHER: "WILL YOU STAY AND
PLAY WITH O. D.?"

PHIL. & VIOLET: "WE WILL!"

MOTHER: "GOOD! I WILL BE HOME
SOON! *(TO O.D)* "O.D. REMEMBER
OUR TALK!"

O. D: "YES MA'AM." *(MOTHER WAVES, EXITS. FRIENDS SIT AND THINK)*

PHILLIP: "WHAT DO YOU WANT TO DO?"

VIOLET: "WE COULD PLAY TAG!"

PHILLIP: "NO, THAT'S BORING."

VIOLET: "JUMP ROPE? *(PHILLIP AND O. D. MAKE FACES)*

O. D: "NOT ME!"

PHILLIP: "ME EITHER! "OH! HEY, I KNOW! LET'S GO TO THE EAST SIDE!"

O. D: "WHAT? UH-UH! NO! I'M NOT GOING!"

PHILLIP: "BUT WHY NOT? LOOK OVER THERE!" *(POINTS)*

VIOLET: "OH-H, IT'S SO PRETTY. *(TO O.D)* "WHY DON'T WE GO?"

O. D: "BECAUSE."

VIOLET: "BECAUSE WHY?

O. D: "OH, JUST BECAUSE…"

PHILLIP: "YES. WE NEED TO GO!"

O. D: "NO!"

VIOLET: "BUT WHY NOT O. D?"

O. D: "MOTHER SAID,NEVER, EVER, EVER, EVER, EVER…!"

PHILLIP: *(SIGHS)* "HEY! JUST SAY IT!"

O. D: "MOTHER SAID NEVER EVER GO TO THE EAST SIDE!"

VIOLET: "OOOOO LOOK! IT'S SO PRETTY! YOU EVER BEEN THERE?"

O. D: "WELL, NO. BUT I LOOK OVER THAT WAY LOTS OF TIMES BEFORE AND THOUGHT ABOUT IT."

VIOLET: "WE SHOULD GO!"

PHILLIP: *(SITS NEAR O.D)* "WE DON'T HAVE TO TELL YOUR MOTHER!"

O. D: "UH-UH!"

VIOLET: "YEAH O.D."

O. D: "BUT THAT'S LYING!"

PHILLIP: "THAT'S NOT LYING!"

VIOLET: "NO. IT'S NOT."

SONG: "THAT'S LYING"

VIOLET: "COME ON O.D!"

O. D: "WELL-L, I DON'T KNOW."

VIOLET: "DON'T BE A DROOPY FLOWER AND NEVER HAVE ANY FUN!"

O. D: "OH-H, (SIGHS)."

PHILLIP: "NOTHING CAN HAPPEN TO US!"

O. D: "I DON'T KNOW," *(THEY PULL HIM UP)*

PHILLIP: "COME ON!"

O.D: "WELL-L!"

SONG: LET'S GO TO THE EAST SIDE"

PHILLIP: "LET'S GO!" *(EXIT)*

SCENE II

(FRIENDS ENTER LOOK AROUND, LOST FANNING, COUGHING. THEY SIGH, ARE SHAKY, SCARED, GAG FROM DRY THROATS, COUGH, HEAR LOUD HOWLING. ALL GRABS, CLING TOGETHER, TREMBLE)

O. D. "YOU HEAR IT?"

PHILLIP/ VIOLET: *(WHISPER)* "UH-HUH! YES!"

VIOLET: "MUST BE MY STOMACH GROWLING."

O.D: "DIDN'T SOUND LIKE IT TO ME."

VIOLET: "MAYBE IT WAS LEAVES FALLING!"

PHILLIP: "LEAVES DON'T SOUND LIKE THAT!"

VIOLET: "YEAH." *(GULP)* "THAT MUST BE IT!"

(SNAKE ENTERS)

SNAKE: *(GROWLS)* "THINK SO, HUH?"

ALL: "OH! AUGH! OOH!" *(PHILLIP, VIOLET DUCK BEHIND O. D)*

O. D: "WHO? WHOOOO…?"

SNAKE: "DON'T LOOK LIKE OWL!" *(GROWLS)*

O.D: "O-OWL?" *(NERVOUS LAUGH)* "NO! N-NOT OWL."

SNAKE: "AW-W, TOO BAD!" *(RUBS HIS STOMACH)* "...LOV-E," *(SLURP)* "OWL! SO DELICIOUS, TENDE... UH," *(COUGHS)* "NICE! YES-S! NICE!"

O. D: "I'M NOT AN OWL! NOT ME!"

PHILLIP: "OR ME!"

VIOLET: "ME EITHER!"

O.D: "WHO ARE YOU?"

SNAKE: "WHY I'M A SNAAA..." *(CLEARS THROAT)* "A SNAA-OBSERVER!"

ALL: *(TOGETHER)* "OH-H?"

PHILLIP: *(PEERS AROUND FRIENDS, VOICE SHAKEY)* "D-DO YOU PLAY ON THE EAST SIDE TOO?"

SNAKE: "NO! I LOOK FOR FOOD!"

VIOLET: "OH, WELL, IT'S PAST OUR DINNERTIME TOO!" *(ALL NOD)*

SNAKE: "I HAVE AN IDEA!" *(PAUSE)* "*ALL OF YOU MUST* STAY *FOR MY DINNER!*"

PHILLIP: "OH-H! UH NO! NO THANKS! WE GOTA LEAVE NOW!" *(SNAKE BLOCKS PATH)*

SNAKE: "OH, DO STAY! MY MEAL IS NOTHING WITHOUT YOU!" *(GROWLS)*

PHILLIP: *(SHOUTS)* "RUN! GO! GET AWAY! RUN FOR YOUR LIFE!"

(ALL RUN, SCATTER, VIOLET, PHILLIP EXIT. O. D. DUCKS INTO A CAVE)

SNAKE: *(SIGH)* "AUGH! TOO BAD THEY GOT AWAY! ALL EXCEPT, YOU…!" *(LAUGHS)*

**SNAKE SINGS
SONG: WELCOME TO MY SIDE OF THE GARDEN**

(SNAKE GRINS BIG AT THE END OF THE SONG)

SCENE III

BACK IN THE GARDEN

(OPOSSUMS ENTER, CARRY VEGETABLES. FLAMINGO, FROG ELEPHANTS, OTHER ANIMALS NEAR)

MOTHER: *(TO HERSELF)* "I DON'T SEE O. D.? I TOLD HIM TO STAY HERE!"

FATHER: "YOU LOOK FOR HIM. I WILL GO IN TO STORE THE FOOD." *(FATHER EXITS)*

MOTHER: *(CALLS)* "O.D!" (*SEES MRS FLAMINGO, SWEEPING, X TO HER)* "MRS. FLAMINGO, HAVE YOU SEEN O. D?"

MS.FLAMINGO: "NO, CAN'T SAY I HAVE DEAR."

MOTHER: "IF YOU DO SEND HIM HOME PLEASE!"

FLAMINGO: "YES, I WILL DEAR."

(MOTHER SEES MR. FROG SUNNING, X TO HIM)

MOTHER: "HELLO MR. FROG!"

MR. FROG: *(CROAK)* "GOOD DAY!"

MOTHER: "DID YOU SEE O. D. TODAY?"

MR. FROG: "NO. BUT I WILL TELL HIM TO GO STRAIGHT HOME IF I DO!"

MOTHER: "THANK YOU!"

FROG: "RE-DEEP!" *(CROAKS)*

MOTHER: "WHERE COULD THEY BE?" *(SEE ELEPHANTS)* " ELEPHANTS! I'LL ASK THEM. *(X)* "EXCUSE ME! HAVE YOU SEEN O. D.?"

MR. ELEPHANT: "NO-O, NOT TODAY!"

MRS. ELEPHANT: "NO DEAR," *(OTHER ANIMALS ENTERS, COME NEAR)* "...NOT SINCE EARLY THIS MORNING." *(MR. OPOSSUM ENTERS)* "I SAW HIM PLAYING WITH HIS FRIENDS." *(POINTS)* "OH! LOOK! THAT'S THEM THERE!"

(PHILLIP, VIOLET ENTER, WINDED, PANTING; RUSH UP TO THE GROUP)

MRS. BEAR: "PHILLIP! VIOLET! WHAT'S THE MATTER?"

MOTHER: "WHERE IS O. D?"

(PHILLIP AND VIOLET FALL TO THE GROUND, EXHAUSTED)

MRS.BEAR: "PHILLIP J. BEAR JR. WHERE HAVE YOU BEEN?"

PHILLIP: *(PANTING)* "OH-H! OH! WE GOT AWAY! THAT THING! ...ON THE EAST SIDE!"

ALL: "EAST SIDE!"

PHILLIP: "WE WERE PLAYING! AND IT…!"

MOTHER: *(INTERRUPTS)* "OH NO! WHERE'S O. D?"

(VIOLET AND PHILLIP LOOK AROUND)

PHILLIP: "HE WAS RIGHT BEHIND US WHEN WE RAN FROM THAT SNAKE!

ALL: "SNAKE!"

MOTHER: *(CRYING)* "OH! NO! I TOLD HIM! NO-O…!"

MOTHER SHEEP: "VIOLET YOU KNOW NOT TO LEAVE THE GARDEN!"

VIOLET: "I'M SORRY MAMA!"

MRS. BUTTERFLY: "LIFE WAS GOOD HERE. BUT THE HUMANS DISOBEYED!"

MR. LYON: "THEY ATE FROM THE FORBIDDEN TREE!"

RABBIT: "AND WERE KICKED OUT OF THE GARDEN!"

ANTELOP: "THEY LEFT US ALL ALONE."

MONKEY: "AND THAT SNAKE..!"

MOTHER: "SNAKE! OH!" *(CRYING)* "NO!" *(LOUD CRYING)*

MONKEY: "GOD TOLD SNAKE TO CRAWL ON HIS BELLY! AND HE SLINKED AWAY TO THE EAST SIDE!"

MOTHER: "**EAST SIDE!** OH NO! O.D'S THERE! WE HAVE TO DO SOMETHING!"

MRS. FLAMINGO: "WE MUST GO AND BRING O. D. HOME!"

MONKEY: "BUT THAT'S DANGEROUS! NOBODY EVER COMES BACK FROM THE EAST SIDE! NOT UNTIL," *(POINTS TO VIOLET AND PHILLIP)* "NO IT'S NOT GOOD TO GO THERE!"

MR. ELEPHANT: "QUIET MONKEY! WE WILL GO! WHO WILL COME WITH ME?"

MOUSE: "ME! I WILL!" *(STEPS FORWARD)*

ALL: "ME TOO! I WANT TO GO! YES! LET'S GO TO GET O.D!"

MR. ELEPHANT: "YES! *(CHANT)* "WE WILL GO!

ALL: "WE WILL GO! WE WILL GO! BRING O. D. HOME! BRING O.D. HOME!" *(ALL CHEER)*

MR. ELEPHANT: "MR. LION!   LEAD US IN PRAYER!"

LION: "YES SIR! LET US PRAY." *(ALL BOW)* "DEAR GOD, PROTECT O. D. KEEP HIM SAFE. AND BE WITH US AS WE GO TO BRING HIM HOME. AMEN."

ALL: "AMEN."

MR. ELEPHANT: "MR FOX!" LINE UP THE VOLUNTEERS!"

MR. FOX: "YES SIR!" VOLUNTEERS! ATTENTION! ALL IN FORMATION!" *(SALUTES)* FOR-WARD! MARCH!"

ALL: " MARCH! MARCH! MARCH! MARCH!" *(REPEAT. GROUP EXITS)*

(ELEPHANT TRUMPETS)

SONG: "WATCH OVER MY CHILD"

MRS. OPOSSUM: *(CALLS)* "BRING O. D. HOME!" *(CRIES; LIGHTS DOWN. SHE EXITS)*

SCENE IV

(O. D. IS TRAPPED IN THE CAVE. SNAKE STIRS BOILING COOKING POT)

O.D: "GO AWAY! I WANT TO GO HOME! I MISS MY MOTHER!"

SNAKE: *(MIMICS O. D)* "I MISS MY MOTHER! QUIET! YOU SHOULD HAVE LISTENED TO HER! OH! WHAT AM I SAYING? THERE WOULD BE NO DINNER FOR ME! NO, YOU DID THE RIGHT THING. I WILL ENJOY YOU! DISOBEDIENT HUH?" *(PAUSE)* "AND A LIAR!" *(LAUGHS)*

O. D: *(CRIES)* "OH-H, YES!"

SNAKE: *(LAUGHS)* "GOOD! I LOVE JUICY MORSELS THAT LIE AND DISOBEY!"

O. D: "I'LL NEVER DO IT AGAIN! NEVER, NEVER, EVER! I'LL NEVER EVER, NEVER!" *(SNAKE LAUGHS)*

SONG: **O. D. AND SNAKES' DUET**

(ELELPHANT'S TRUMPET CALL)

SNAKE: "WHAT'S THAT?"

O. D: *(CRYING)* "I DON'T KNOW!"

SNAKE: "WHATEVER IT IS I DON'T WANT IT TO SPOIL MY DINNER!" *(TRUMPET SOUND)* "I BETTER HIDE!" *(HIDES, PEEKS OUT ELEPHANT, OTHERS ENTER)* "OH! IT'S THAT ELEPHANT!"

O. D: *(SEE FRIENDS)* "YOO-HOO! HERE I AM! HELP ME!" *(POINTS)* "THERE HE IS! OVER THERE!"

SNAKE: "SHHH! HUSH!"

ELEPHANT: *(TO O. D)* "O. D. STAY THERE! LET US TAKE CARE OF HIM!"

O. D: *(CRYING)* "OH, THAT THING…!"

ELEPHANT: *(TO O.D)* "EVERYTHING IS FINE." *(TO SNAKE)* "GO! EAT FROM THE GROUND LIKE YOU WERE TOLD!"

SNAKE: "NOBODY TOLD ANY OF YOU TO COME! I WAS KICKED OUT OF THE GARDEN AND CAME HERE! I NEVER INVITED YOU!"

(ELEPHANT LOOKS UP AT THE GLISTENING COLORS ON THE MOUNTAIN SIDE)

ELEPHANT: *(TO SNAKE)* "SO-O! THAT'S HOW YOU DID IT. THAT'S HOW YOU GOT SO MANY TO COME HERE! LOOK!" *(POINTS TO MOUNTAIN)* "YOU KNEW THEY COULD SEE THE BEAUTIFUL BRIGHT COLORS AND WOULD COME! THAT'S HOW YOU TRAPPED DINNER! WELL-L THAT'S THE LAST MEAL YOU'LL GET FROM THE GARDEN!"

SNAKE: *(PLEADS)* "OH, I'M TIRED OF EATING FRUIT! I NEED PROTEIN!"

ELEPHANT: "TOO BAD!" *(STOMPS)* "GO! GIT!"

(SNAKE HANGS HIS HEAD, EXITS)

RACCOON: *(TO O.D.)* "YOU CAN COME OUT O. D."

O. D: *(EXITS CAVE)* "HERE I AM!"

RACCOON: "YOU'RE ALL RIGHT NOW!"

O.D: "YES! OOF!" *(HAND ON HEART)* "EXCEPT THAT MY HEART IS BEATING REALLY, REALLY FAST!"

BEAR: "I KNOW SON. YOU ARE SAFE NOW. BUT YOU DID SOMETHING WRONG."

O. D: *(NODS)* "UH HUH."

BEAR: "YOU DISOBEYED."

TIGER: "…AND LIED."

ELEPHANT: "YOU WENT TO A PLACE YOU WERE TOLD NOT TO GO."

O. D. "I KNOW." *(BOWS HIS HEAD)* "BUT I'LL NEVER DO IT AGAIN! NEVER EVER, EVER…"

TIGER: *(INTERRUPTS)* "O. D! YOU PROMISED YOUR PARENTS YOU

WOULD NOT GO TO THE EAST SIDE, BUT HERE YOU ARE."

O. D. "YES."

SPIDER: YOU DISOBEYED SOMEONE ELSE TOO."

O. D. *(PAUSE)* "GOD."

RACCOON: "THAT'S RIGHT. YOU NEED TO PRAY AND ASK HIMTO FORGIVE YOU." *(O. D. NODS)*

ELEPHANT: "O. D., YOU CAME LOOKING FOR SOMETHING YOU ALREADY HAVE AT HOME. THESE COLORS ARE JUST REFLECTIONS OF THE GARDEN'S OWN BEAUTY. THIS MOUNTAINSIDE JUST MIRRORS THE GARDEN COLORS."

O. D. "THESE ARE THE SAME COLORS WE HAVE IN THE GARDEN?"

ELEPHANT: "YES! IT'S RIGHT

THERE FOR US ALL TO ENJOY.
AND WE DON'T HAVE TO
COME HERE TO FIND IT."

O. D "I HAVE A GOOD HOME
AND EVERYTHING I COULD
EVER WANT THERE."

ELEPHANT: "YES! WE DON'T
HAVE TO LEAVE TO FIND
WHAT WE NEED. EVERYTHING
GOOD IS RIGHT THERE. O. D., YOUR
PARENTS ARE WAITING! MR FOX!
GET EVERYONE TOGETHER AND
LET'S GO HOME!"

MR. FOX: "YES SIR
ATTENTION! EVERYBODY!
GET IN FORMATION!" *(ALL LINE UP)*

ELEPHANT: *(TO O. D. AND ALL)* "LET'S
GO HOME!"

MR. FOX: "FORWARD! MARCH!
MARCH! MARCH! MARCH...!"

(ELEPHANT'S TRUMPET CHANT)

SCENE V

(MONKEY SITS ON PERCH VIEWING THE PATH)

MONKEY: *(SEES ELEPHANT, CALLS)* **"SCREECH, SCREECH! SCREECH!"**

(OPOSSUMS, ALL ANIMALS ENTER)

MOTHER: *(SEES, CALLS)* "O. D.! O. D.! *(RUNS TO HIM)*

MR. OPOSSUM: "O. D! ARE YOU ALL RIGHT?

O.D: "MAMA! POPPA!" *(NODS)* "YES!" (HUGS) "I'M SORRY! I DISOBEYED." *(PARENTS NOD)* "I'LL PRAY AND ASK GOD TO FORGIVE ME."

MOTHER: "GOOD SON!"

FATHER: "DON'T FORGET TO THANK OUR FRIENDS FOR BRINGING

YOU BACK HOME."

O. D. "YES, I WILL." *(TO FRIENDS)* "THANK YOU ALL FOR COMING TO GET ME."

ALL: "YOU'RE WELCOME!
YOU ARE HOME NOW; AND YOU ARE SAFE!"

FATHER: "SON, IT'S LATE. AND WE HAVE TO GO HOME."

O. D. "YES POPA. MAY I STAY AND SAY GOODNIGHT TO VIOLET AND PHILLIP?"

FATHER: "YES. BUT COME IN AFTER YOU DO. WE HAVE TO TALK."

O. D: "YES SIR."

MOTHER: "WE'RE GLAD
YOU ARE HOME SAFE." (HUG)
(VILLAGERS, PARENTS WAVE, EXIT)

PHILLIP: "O.D. WE'RE SORRY."
(VIOLET NODS)

O. D: "THAT'S ALL RIGHT."

PHILLIP: "ARE WE STILL FRIENDS?"

O. D: "YES."

VIOLET: "THANKS O. D."

PHILLIP: "YES THANKS. I HAVE TO GO HOME."

VIOLET: "ME TOO! SEE YOU TOMORROW O. D." *(FRIENDS EXIT)*

(O. D. WAVES GOODBYE, SINGS)
SONG: FORGIVE ME LORD

(ALL RE-ENTER SINGING)
SONG: "IN OUR GARDEN"

(END)

Sue L. Adkins

Production Information
From Sue L. Adkins

Note: Speaking Parts can be assigned as written, or spoken lines can be stacked and spoken by other than designated characters in the original script. This play is written so there can be flexibility in casting. Parts and lines can be assigned at the discretion of the director. The original production was done with a pre-teen youth choir of thirty children, but a smaller group can perform this production. The play can be performed by ages 5-12 years old, and by adults for children. Running time: approximately 35 minutes.

Characters:
O. D. Opossum
Mother & Father Opossum
Phillip J. & Mother & Father Bear
Violet, Mother & Father Sheep
Monkey (A boy or girl)
Mr. & Mrs. Elephant
Mrs. Flamingo
Mr. Frog
Raccoon
Mrs. Butterfly
Mr. Tiger
Rabbit
Mr. Fox
Lion
Spider
Zebra
Mouse I; Little Mouse
Antelope
(You can have several of some animals if you have a large group)

Props: Plastic Fruit; Broom (Ms Flamingo); Dry Ice for Snake's cooking pot. (Optional), A stirring stick (Nothing sharp); Sun glasses (Mr. Frog), Lounge chair (Mr. Frog, optional); Apron (Mrs. Opossum). Plastic gardening tools, scaled-down watering hose, basket for flowers. (Optional)

Watering Can and other props as indicated. Weaved grass or vine mats, bag to hold food Mother and father Opossum gather.

Costumes: Animal costumes: Can be simple head dresses only, or more elaborate full dress costumes. *Be creative.* <u>Caution!</u> Head dress and gear should not obstruct child's vision. Costumes should be a safe length, not cumbersome, or risk causing them to trip. Big bulky costumes can be a hazard. <u>Safety First!</u>

Lights: Lighting can range from elaborate to basic house lights; turning them up or down as scene indicated. *Always provide enough light to get children on and off the playing area with safety.

Set: The playing area can be done in various ways. If there is a stage, the "Garden" should make up approx. 2/3's of the area. The East side can be approximately 1/3 of the playing area and setup down right or left stage. Floor aisles can also be used as entrances and exits. The playing area can be set with artificial plants and trees to indicate the "Garden;" with a center circle area or raised point to place a camouflaged or hidden bench, stool, step ladder hidden by plants and trees to serve as monkey's perch. Children can remain seated in garden area. They become the choir as action takes place on the Eastside.

Scenes by Songs:

"In Our Garden"
Lights up: Animals enter L, R and or from audience aisle; actors mime pruning plants, sweeping, talking, watering plants; sing and greet. Most animal characters become the chorus, at song end they cross, some waving, move into position, there to sing on cue.

"Don't Eat The Fruit"
O. D. enters left, rushes, cross (x) up center. Some neighbors enter right, wave, X left, some exit. Other villagers exit right. O. D. spots fruit on ground near trees; cross (x), gets fruit on ground. Mother enters; X rushes over to stops him from eating.

O-B-E-Y: OBEY THE LORD
Mother Opossum reminds O. D. to obey God.

"THAT'S LYING"
O. D.'s friends try get him to do wrong.

"LET'S GO TO THE EAST SIDE"
Phillip and Violet talk O.D. into going to the East Side.

"WELCOME TO MY SIDE OF THE GARDEN"
Snake captures O. D. and teases him.

"O. D. AND SNAKE'S DUET"
O. D. laments coming to the East Side.

"ELEPHANTS' CHANT"
Chorus chant, hums, Elephant makes a loud trumpet sound.

"FORGIVE ME"
O. D. thanks God, asks for forgiveness and for himself, and his friends.

Character and Scene Sketches

Set: Can be done in a circular fashion with greenery and foliage. It can be divided with two-thirds of the area set as the Garden and one-third as the Eastside. Monkey's perch can be set down R or L of the garden area. Up L of the garden is the meadow of trees, and the forbidden Fruit Tree. Down R or L of center area is a fashioned pond with lily pad attached and spaced to appear in a floating effect.

Characters: O. D. Opossum; Mother, Father Opossum; Phillip J. Bear (O. D's best friend) Violet Ewe: O. D's friend. A sheep (Ewe) costume: Pinafore, hair ribbon; Mother & Father Opossum; Snake: (Long thin mincing devilish serpent) Mr. & Mrs. Elephant; Mrs. Flamingo; Mother Sheep; Father Bear; Monkey.

Other Suggested Characters: Butterfly, Lion, Rabbits, Zebra, Mice, Tiger, Fox, Raccoon, Spider, Antelope. Add or limit cast number according to number of children available.

PROPS: Broom: Apron (optional); Sun glasses; small lounge chair; boiling pot and stirring stick;

After The Beginning The Play

Other Cheudi Publications

Life Lessons
By Henry O. Adkins

After The Beginning In The Garden
By Sue Adkins

Raising Great Kids
By Henry and Sue Adkins

Celebrating Kwanzaa
By Sue Adkins

Out Of The Corner Of My Eye
By Sue Adkins

String Town
By Sue Adkins

My Bible A B C's
By Henry O. Adkins

Inspirational/Children Play

Sue L. Adkins is an author of Children's books with music, a playwright and actress. She is a graduate of Texas Woman's University and Southern Methodist University Graduate School. She lives in Plano, Texas with husband Henry. They have three children.

This play shows us why it is good to obey and tell the truth. We must also pray, and be ready to forgive. An example is told in story and songs. We pray that these lessons will become a part of the lives of all who perform, see, and hear this work. We hope it will make you think and influence you and others in a positive way.

Sue L. Adkins

ISBN 0-9672605-7-4

Cheudi Publishing, P.O. Box 940572,
Plano, Texas 75094

www.ingramcontent.com/pod-product-compliance
Lightning Source LLC
Chambersburg PA
CBHW072036060426
42449CB00010BA/2300